You Are Fired Said The Heart To The Ego

Ed Rychkun

ISBN 978-0-9782623-7-2

Copyright© 2008 Ed Rychkun

If you feel it is necessary to quote or use the material in this book, please do so but the condition is that you refer people to my website at www.edrychkun.com and you simply provide a reference to me whenever and if ever you use the material.

Editing: Hope Rychkun
Cover design: Manoj Sharma
www.indyahub.com

A Private Limited Liability Enterprise

CONTENTS

INTRODUCTION

YES, EGO YOU ARE FIRED

I ONLY TAKE ORDERS SAYS THE BRAIN

WHY DID YOU WAKE ME ASKS THE MIND?

WHO CALLS ME ASKS THE SOUL?

AND IS GOD PRESENT?

AND SOUL SHALL EXPLAIN

THE CHAKRA CHILDREN SPEAK

NEW CONSCIOUSNESS AWAKENS

INTRODUCTION

What is it that makes us tick? Why do we struggle to understand who we are? Why do we think we know all there is to know? Why does life need to be a struggle? Do you care? Is there more to our life than we could comprehend?

Yes, many questions. Are there many answers? No it is actually very simple if you know how to die temporarily and come back. Or perhaps if you could use intuition the way it was intended? Sound like severe and strange alternatives? Why don't you indulge in a discussion with the Ego, the Heart, the Mind, the Brain and the Soul and see what they figure out?

These are all questions which used to perplex me. I think now, after how many lifetimes I am yet to discover, the answers are simple. They are in this little book.

See if your intuition is tuned in to the same frequency.

Ed Rychkun

YES, EGO YOU ARE FIRED

"You are fired," said the Heart to the Ego, "you have been measured, you have been weighed and you have been found wanting."

"And who may you be to make such threats to me?" replied the Ego.

"I am Heart. I lie here in this body and I am in desperate need of attention. As the central engine to this body, I have weakened rapidly and I am not able to do my duties of supplying blood and oxygen to the body. Blood pressure is high, arteries are becoming plugged, and many organs are becoming weak and on the verge of failure. My life is drawing near to an end. I have had a stroke and am unable to fulfill my duties."

"How is it that you speak with me, Heart? We do not normally speak to each other."

"Ego, it is my final moment of desperation that a window of direct communication has opened between us. As we do not see each other, we know we each exist, sense, and communicate through this body's subtle energy architecture. What does it matter, anyway?"

"So why are you bothering me?" asked the Ego.

"It is because you have stressed this poor body by deluging it with needs for betterment, more power, more money and created such a fear of loss and poor self-worth that the anxiety has manifested itself in serious problems I cannot cope with. In addition, because you are constantly building desires for excessive food and drink, and easy living, this body has become unhealthy, contaminated and saturated with poisons. It is you that must stop this or we will both perish."

"Look, Heart," the Ego replied, "I am doing my job. If you can't handle yours, then that is your concern. What am I to do about it?"

"Ego, answer these questions for me. Are you very compassionate, understanding, and generous? Are the emotions of love, joy, happiness, honesty, and respect very important to you? Are you considerate and sensitive to the needs of others, and empathetic to their pain? Are you able to feel love for all beings around you, in an ever-widening circle from yourself and family, friends, neighbors, countrymen, fellow human beings and all living things on Earth? Do you ever see the Divine in all beings, and do you realize the same Self in you is also the Self in them as well?"

"My job is to protect the human I am assigned to. I am responsible for keeping you and your physical form, and the body from harm or need. I am here to make sure that the human has all its needs and desires looked after. The human requires guidance on how to create a comfortable existence in the future and insure it has what it needs from the past to best survive in satisfaction and comfort. It must not be hurt in any way. That, Heart, is my job and I take it serious, thank you."

"Ego, I am the center of Love and Compassion. Your methods are destructive to that purpose. Look at me. You have been measured by me and you are full of negative thoughts involving hatred, guilt, selfishness, paranoia, impatience, anger, fear and self-pity. You can have powerful, passionate thoughts for others, but you will only love another or do something for them on the condition that they love or do something for you first. You are stone hearted, unsympathetic, and self-centered. You are afraid to love others, and unable to love yourself. How is that a way to protect this being from harm?"

"What concern is it of yours how I perform my duties? If you and the body cannot handle the pressure, then that is too bad. You must adjust or perish."

"Ego, what gives you the right to make such a decision? The concern is that your actions of energy affect the thought system of this human. And this drives the emotions and feelings which create dis-ease and dysfunction in the body. I, as a physical part of this human am constantly fooled by your misguided protection, sending signals to my counterpart the Brain to trigger enzymes and hormones created by fear and anger. These are destructive and I am weakening. I have told you I cannot pump blood fast enough. I cannot transfer oxygen into the blood fast enough. This, as I have pointed out to you, has now resulted in poor circulation, hypertension, contaminated blood, dysfunctional liver, pancreas… must I go on?"

"So why do you do it, if you are so compassionate and full of love. Have you gone dysfunctional yourself?"

"I can only send a signal out based upon what you and the Mind and its energy system tells me. You create fear and anxiety, not me. You create the instructions to the Brain to trigger these emotions. I can only relate what I am told.

You are the guilty one that needs to have your position changed."

"And what gives you the authority to change my position?"

"I am in charge of the central life support system. I am the center of love. I am in constant communications with the Soul and I am the portal to Spirit. I reflect what is in the heart which is supposed to be goodness and unconditional love. I am a reflector of emotion and I have but one choice in sending the signal to the brain that will release the appropriate chemistry for the emotion. You do not listen. Your influence has brought about emotional issues of conditional love, lack of compassion, low confidence, lack of inspiration, no hope, despair, hate, envy, fear, jealousy, anger, and lack of generosity into this human's life. You create distrust, hate, conflict, anxiety and fear in this human forcing it to generate such negative emotional energy through me. That is what is causing a serious deterioration."

"So what? The human needs to be aware of these so it can better its life. At any rate, what you say does not give you authority over me."

"I have reported my condition to my Superior as I will, assuming the stroke is averted, rapidly fall to physical dysfunctions such as heart conditions, diabetes, asthma, lung & breast cancers, thoracic spine, pneumonia, upper back, and shoulder problems. These are already prevalent in this body. Is that enough?"

"That is your problem. The human does not take issue with my work so my performance is not an issue!"

"You have been given the opportunity of choice to manage as you see fit. You have without regards to the body decided on your own to do what you deem important. You have become over zealous with your importance. You have failed in your job and now you must report to me first before anything goes to the Brain."

"And who is this Superior you speak of that will force me to do this?"

"It is the Mind. It communicates to you and it has your counterpart of Soul to communicate to. It is the same as the Higher Self or Spiritual part of our makeup that is designed to manage this body while on this planet."

"And how do you propose I am to work with you?" asked the Ego.

"The human's spiritual language is through emotion. When the human has thoughts of goodness, compassion, love and charity it generates emotions that are coherent, strong and in harmony. I am a ball of energy reaching outwards. When this is strong, the Brain is able to feel the harmonics and respond with the appropriate reactions that govern the anatomy and chemistry of the human. If the human feels fear, anger, confusion or conflict, the result is that incoherent harmonics are sent, creating discord and discomfort in the human. You and your protection method create discord and a destructive environment by using the Mind to serve your own purpose, interfering with the chemistry, and ignoring the Soul. I must filter your thoughts and intents before they create discourse."

"Look here," replied the Ego, "I advise the human on every matter. This brings things into its Mind where it can protect itself. Are you telling me that I have to ask you first?"

"From now on, should you decide to create negative thoughts, you must check with me first. These thoughts must first be approved by me and they must be filtered from negative to positive before they are received by the Brain, either from you or the Mind."

"And if I do not?"

"Then the human, if it survives the current state, will rapidly fall into negative dysfunction and be prone to disease as is the case now. We lie here in a heart stroke situation. As I have manifested the ills of your influence, we will simply cease to exist, or this will accelerate or occur again until death to us all. If you believe that you should properly serve the human, then you should be willing to use me as your filter in the best interest of the human."

"I have no reason to believe you can do any better."

"That is your prerogative. As you continue to inflict negative energy, the human will die so you will be out of a job anyway."

"Ok, but you already give directives to the Brain, as you say through emotion, and who only knows what else. What assurance have I that you can do a better job? And what does the Brain have to say about this? It is your counterpart in the body. Should it not have something to say about this?"

I ONLY TAKE ORDERS SAYS THE BRAIN

"Ok, ok, look you two," responded the Brain. "I have been listening to you both and you have to also understand my position. I simply take orders which come in as energy signals and directives from you. I am in no position to choose which one is better, wrong or right. How can I? These are simply signals."

"Well," replied the Heart, "do you want to send bad directives to the body and make it impossible to function, and then die?"

"No," said the Brain, "but are you aware that it is the emotion that creates a reaction in me that affects the body? I want to explain something about this body you are in to you both. The ANS, short for Autonomic Nervous System, kicks into action upon any threat that works in two parts. First is the fight or flight situation where the sympathetic system causes the body to constrict blood vessels, raise blood pressure, raise heart rate, constrict skin arteries, move blood away from organs, dilate pupils, and raise neck hairs for starters. And this is all done automatically in a few seconds to prepare the human for action if needed. I create the orders to do this. That is part of my job."

"Yes, we are aware of this." the Heart responded.

"Then?"

"All right," answered the Brain, "the second situation is when the threat is only perceived like when the body walks into a dark alley and feels threatened. Then the parasympathetic system kicks in. It causes the heart rate to go up, creates a sweat, or chill, and the blood pressure goes up in readiness. So I have to also give an order to you the Heart to do that, got it?"

"Yes," said the Heart, "I understand that."

"When that happens me and our friend Ego must do our job. The hormonal system – neurohormonal – starts a long sequence of reactions of nervous system signals to the glands so as to increase chances of survival and these take a few minutes but they last for hours. This is a big responsibility and requires some 1400 reactions to occur in the body."

"Like what?" the Heart responded.

"Listen carefully. It's like when the body is wounded or something. There are a lot of things that have to happen so the body can protect itself. For example, I have to send a signal to release cortisol from the adrenals when we perceive such stress – just like being wounded. It goes into the blood to raise blood sugar so muscles have more fuel. Adrenaline increases to increase the heart beat, and it also raises blood pressure by constricting arteries and interacting with kidneys to save salt and water. So this is what the protective system does automatically and I have to make sure that it is so."

"But here is the root of the problem," Heart responded. "This same process is also triggered by negative emotion like anger, fear and depression that has nothing to do with a real flight or fright situation. Does this not create a feedback loop of stress, then cortisol, then bad mood, more stress, and more cortisol that can reach a burnout condition? And does this cortisol that you launch not inhibit memory, clarity, and higher functions of the brain, and the body? And what about the other 1399 functions you trigger?"

"Well, you tell me how I am supposed to know whether the threat is true or untrue. How am I supposed to now the difference? If Ego or you send me a directive as a result of fear, I must obey. Nobody gives me qualifications as to whether it is real or not. I may work up here in the attic but I simply take and execute orders."

"Well, you are aware that emotions caused by fear can be fake. But what about the emotions created by anxiety, hate and stress? They are producing the same signals that you may be misdirecting? Are you aware that emotions like love, compassion, gratitude, and joy stop these negative buildups that you create and dissipate the problems you create in the body?"

"So, Heart, once again, how am I to know the difference? I am simply a computer in the attic. Ask this Ego why it sends these signals to me if they are inappropriate."

"I am."

"Look, you two," replied Ego, "if you want to make a big deal about this cortisol, the body has built in things to counteract. DHEA is another hormone by adrenals actually that counteracts the effects of cortisol."

"Right," answered the Heart, "but it is produced by positive emotions of love, compassion, gratitude, and joy? And you know that this hormone declines with age, so you need to do something about it now because a stress button can get stuck in the on position."

"Well, this body is getting upset about things like finances, job, conflict, and anxiety problems. These are stress triggers that accumulate on an ongoing basis. If the body gets used to a new threshold, and the cortisol and adrenaline are stuck in the on positions, what am I supposed to do about it?"

"Well Ego," said the Heart, "that is my very point. You said you were here to protect the body. You are heartless and have no conscience in how you apply your goals. You need to put me, the Heart into your process. Does heart disease, raised blood sugar, hypertension, high cholesterol, obesity, arterial diseases, and diabetes over time sound like protection? What happens when the body functions get set to a new higher dangerous threshold as the body simply believes this is where it should be, then burns out early, like now? Do you, the Brain support this?"

"Well, no," replied the Brain, "of course I don't want to cease existence and make things difficult. But are you understanding that I simply take orders from you two which I convert to action, and I don't know the difference. You just send energy signals to me and my job is to do as I am told."

"Ok, I see that," answered the Heart, "but Ego, let me ask you this: Who do you receive your guidance from? You certainly don't listen to me."

"Well, I receive my guidance from the Mind. But the Mind never complains about what I do. So what is the problem here? Does the Mind not represent you and the Soul? If the Mind does not say anything to me, and lets me do as I am doing,

I can only assume it agrees that I have to be doing a great job."

"Well, that is where we have a problem. You are wanting. You are the one that has this human worried about a future, wanting to be better than others, have more money, more power, bigger this, bigger that, fearful about loss, protecting this and that. And are you not the one that is always on the shoulder making sure that you, the 'Ego is not hurt'? Is that your job?"

"Of course it is. I am making it a better, more comfortable place for this body to exist in. I have to ensure that it can reproduce, protect, provide and control its life going forward."

"At the expense of the body?"

"Look, these things make the human feel better, look better, and have a quality life. That is my job! Bodies all die at some stage, get used to that reality."

"But Ego, why can't you find a better balance. Why not try to reset the thermostat down to a normal level again because this stress can become an addiction. If a diet of positive feelings resolve this problem and this is how you can reset the thermostat, why not bring these into the directives? The human may live longer and have less stress."

"Look, that's all iffy. I do what I do!" screamed the Ego, "I provide joy and all that good feeling stuff by focusing on getting better, nicer things, and a more comfortable life. You don't seem to get it. And no one complains, do they?"

"Ok you guys," interjected the Brain. "I want you to know I am just the order taker in the attic and I certainly support a better life for this body, as it would certainly make my life less chaotic, but can I ask you something?"

"Go ahead," the Heart mumbled.

"As I understand things, you, the Heart also send out many orders to me, independent of Ego. Is the heart area not the real core? Is it not the real control center? Are these sayings like heartfelt emotion, heartbroken, put your heart into it, the heart of the matter, heart to heart, and from the bottom of my heart just meaningless sayings? Are they not reflecting a real process from the heart center – chakras and the heart's own field? And do you not send signals in this regards?"

"Yes," the Heart responded, "that is so."

"Look, I am no dummy," continued the Brain, "I know you have a heart signal that is 50 times stronger in amplitude than mine. I know this field of yours can reach eight feet away and one can hear your beat that far away. And I also receive those waves from you up here through the ANS system. I know that the source of heartbeat or pacemaker is you, and sure messages that regulate speed comes to you through the ANS from me, but the heartbeat is independent of the brain. Is this true?"

"Yes, it is," answered the Heart, "but I can be influenced by you when you need to vary the heart rate in order to meet perceived fake demands from you and Ego."

"Fair enough, then why don't you do your job and generate better emotional signals to me?"

"Ok, now we are back to the crux of the matter. You can both influence me and force me to do things just as you must take your directives. This is where Ego starts interfering with things creating fake perceived conflicts and stress demands. And if you decide to make me beat faster, how can I say no?"

"Fair enough," replied the Brain. "we seem to have a conflict and overlap of responsibilities between all of us."

"Yes," continued the Heart, "emotional states affect the heart rate variability. Yes, when stress hits or negative emotions occur, I go chaotic like an earthquake graph. And yes, I am coherent and send nice smooth signals in deep sleep or sincere positive emotions. And yes, this is what creates improved clarity, mood, and communications."

"And," the Brain continued, "is it not true that the signals go from you to the survival centre in the hindbrain where blood pressure, heart rate, and respiratory rate are controlled? This part analyses the information and makes changes. These signals also affect your feelings and emotional memory center in midbrain called an amygdala. The cells here synchronize to the pacemaker in the heart. If the heart rate is chaotic, it matches that to negative emotional experiences and automatically recalls what negative feeling correlates. Brain waves in the cortex are also affected by powerful chaotic heart signals coloring how the human will think and perceive, altering top level functions like communications, calculation, planning, creativity, and other functions – all from the big signal generator below in the heart! So why don't you get your shit together and do your job?"

"Well, I have to repeat, it is the Ego that wants to do it a different way. You must understand that I am an organ that takes orders like you. You are in the attic and I am in the operations center but we are simply physical puppets to the Ego. It calls the shots along with what the body perceives as real through the Mind. Yes, emotions have to change by reversing stress. I need to get out of chaotic mode to stop sending signals to you so you don't respond to anxiety, panic, and anger directives. Yes, I have the power called heart intelligence but I can't really use it while Ego plays its game of subjective survival."

"Look, you two physical dummies," drummed the Ego, "you are here to respond to what I tell you. I am doing my job! Period. And if anybody should be fired it is you two belly-achers for trying to cause more tension and anxiety."

"Hold it a minute," queried the Brain, "it seems to me that the Ego is a construct, an invisible energy field which is really not part of the body. It is part of the Mind, is it not? And if the Heart can send me orders as can the Ego, is this not a problem of conflicting responsibilities? Is that not the real issue? Ego says he reports to the Mind and the Mind is happy. Who does the Heart report to? Is it not the Mind as well?"

WHY DID YOU WAKE ME ASKS THE MIND?

"What's all this chatter going on? Why have you three awoken me?" muttered the Mind. "I was having a restful sleep."

"Mind, we are sorry to wake you but there is a conflict here. Are you in charge of the Ego and what the Heart feels?" the Brain and the Heart asked simultaneously?

"Of course I am. Is there some problem?"

"Yes," said Ego, "this big dummy called the Heart is accusing me of giving the Brain bad instructions that destroy the body. I am performing my job and it wants to fire me. It says I have been found wanting and becoming dysfunctional as a result. It says we are in perish mode as it has had a stroke."

"Yes, that is correct." said the Heart.

"Well, really" replied the Mind, "that is serious. The Ego, by design, has a primary purpose of protecting the body from threats and insuring that it manifest a safe existence by directing the bottom three chakras of survival, reproduction, and power."

"Does it not have to balance that responsibility in any way so the body does not fall victim to disease and dysfunction?" asked the Heart.

"Yes."

"Well," pressed the Heart, "Ego has accentuated a duality by constantly bringing thoughts about competition, protection, betterment and other survival mechanisms as an urgent desire for material possessions first and foremost. Does this not have to go through you, the Mind, before the Brain is given directives? If these directives and emotion falls strongly to the dark side with thoughts and feelings of fear, anger, and hostility, it results in the Brain creating unwanted reactions in the body. These are destructive to longevity and happiness. Don't you filter this if you are in charge?"

"Why do I need to filter it?"

"Because I have a problem in that I am deteriorating rapidly, had a stroke and affecting the health and longevity of the body. I also give directives to the Brain as a result of the emotion that Ego creates through his neglect. If the actions of Ego are misguided and fall to the dark side, because it favors a goal of evolving morals around competition, protection, survival, with little regards to balance with the light side, is this your idea of proper protection? The Ego has effectively dominated the evolutionary plan and has gone beyond its responsibilities, has it not? Or is this what you encourage?"

"No, because I also must balance things with the Soul."

"Well what does the Soul have to say about this?"

"Well, look at this first. The Soul is directly connected to the Heart through the Chakra system which also can give the Body directives through the subtle energies. So you see there are actually four areas that can affect the body either adversely or constructively. It is not just the Heart, the Brain, and the Ego. I don't have any authority over the Soul or the Chakras, do any of you?"

"Mind, you are avoiding the question," affirmed Heart, "you said you check with the Soul as part of your job."

"Yes," answered Mind hesitantly, "but I thought everything was going well and I have no need to contact Soul."

"If this is so, then it is even more difficult for the Brain and me," said the Heart. "This is even worse than I thought. What about the upper three chakras that the Ego overrides, limiting the growth on the spiritual side and losing a proper balance between upper and lower chakras? Not only does the Ego screw me up by generating bad emotions, it gives its own directives to the Brain, and on top of that represses the top chakras to limit any spiritual growth that can balance the bottom three chakras. The whole thing is skewed by Ego and you say everything is well? Why do you need authority over the Soul? Why not just ask? Does this stroke sound like all is well?"

"Yes, that is true," replied the Mind, "I do have authority over the Ego and I do represent the Soul as well. And I can indeed influence what you and Brain do as well. But you do understand that you both have other direct responsibilities that I cannot influence and there may be a hazy line between responsibilities and divisions."

"Well," drummed the Heart, "my question is simple. Where is the Soul in this picture? You have been sleeping so long that the Soul's silent proddings have been ignored. The Soul is not going to demand anything and make a loud noise. Should you not ask the Soul or me to filter thoughts before they become negative actions? You obviously can't have asked the Soul anything before an intent to create emotion in me is demanded. I know enough that this state of fear, greed and crushing stress is not in the design of Soul's purpose."

"Look, Heart," replied the Mind with raised voice, "are you saying I am incompetent and not doing my job?"

"Just look at the state of the body," answered the Heart. "Is that what you want? You have been asleep, so how could you be paying any attention to what the Ego is doing or what Soul really wants? Answer me that."

"Ok, ok," mumbled the Mind, "I may have been asleep for a while but as I said, I can't control the chakra system, Soul, you or the Brain completely. It is controlled from outside – through Spirit. How can I control the automatic survival instincts that the Brain controls? Furthermore, how can I balance things on behalf of Soul when there is free choice? On top of that, there is another issue here. What about when you yourself send directives to the Brain and ignore Ego – and me? Me, the Mind is a small part of this system. Sure I can manage the Ego and the Soul so that things are filtered through the Heart but that is only part of it. No one can control human Consciousness that can choose whether it abides by, Ego, or the Soul. It can override things just like Ego can override the Heart. On the other hand, the Heart can override the Brain and you can both override the Soul. And you can all override the energy systems within you – the chakras. So you see, it is not just a simple matter of laying blame on me or anyone in particular."

"You mean no one has the power to manage this all properly?" said the Heart despondently.

"Well," answered the Mind, "consider what 'properly' means? What is proper to each of you? You are all trying to do a job and you do have conflicting responsibilities when you consider this notion of what is proper. What do you want, long life, money, power, peace, joy, harmony, conflict, or what? Each has a different need, action, directive, and judgment attached. So do you all make judgments based on your own requirements? Which of you is to say what is wrong or right for the human? And finally, think about what the Soul has in its life design for it to do. Have you given that any consideration before you flap about blaming others?"

"It seems to me," said Ego, "that giving this human a good life is proper where survival is guaranteed, it has power and abundance and all the things that make it happy. That's what I do, and will continue to do."

"It seems to me," said the Heart, "that the human should be healthy and happy and live a long life without any conflict, anger or fear. All you do is give it stress and anxiety."

"It seems to me," said the Mind, "that you two don't have the proper perspective about the real purpose of the human and the body. Sure I have been asleep and haven't had a management meeting for quite a while, but this human is free to make its choices, isn't it."

"It seems to me," said the Brain, "that for me to give proper non-conflictive directives, you three should get together so the body is in better harmony. How am I supposed to know what to do when there are several areas of responsibility, like chakras, Mind, Heart and now this Consciousness to take orders from? No wonder the human is dysfunctional and gets diseases."

"You all make your points," said the Mind, "but in the end, I have to reinforce that it is the Human Consciousness that has the last choice. It is what controls all of us."

"Mind, you are once again avoiding the issues. Consciousness cannot control the Soul, none of us can. Anyway, why do we need to bring Consciousness into this? We are talking about managing thoughts and emotions. They come into Consciousness through your action of bringing to Mind," the Heart responded sheepishly.

"True," said the Mind, "I must qualify that no one of us can control the Soul. Yes, I can choose what is brought into Consciousness, as I can choose to take advice from the Soul. And then it can advise me to act accordingly. But I have not heard from Soul."

"Well where is this Consciousness?" asked the Heart, "We need to have a discussion with it."

"But what is it?" asked the Brain. "And where is it? I thought Consciousness was you, the Mind and what you bring into it, as Heart has suggested."

"Ok," said the Heart despondently, "this is getting us nowhere. We are now pointing a finger to the Soul and Consciousness. The Brain says it is doing its job and only takes orders. The Ego says the same, the Mind admits some negligence in sleeping but it controls thoughts and intent which controls us. Then it says we have other considerations such as Consciousness and the Chakra energy centers. Where does this end? In the meantime, I am about to die because this human can't take the stress, fear and anxiety of what the Ego calls a good life. This cannot be right."

"What do you propose?" asked the Mind. "Do you have any ideas on what is right?"

"I am tired and unwell as you have all made me so. Yet I am the Heart, I am the physical organ of Creation. I am unconditional love and compassion. I represent the Zero or Balancing point of the human system you have been representing in your duties. The three Chakras relating to the physical world are below me and the three above are three Chakras relating to the *internal* representation of the physical world or the Soul. I am governed by the Sun, and I am known by the emerald color green. My main message of the Heart is that of balance and interconnection between self-love and love for others. I am telling you that you have all been found wanting in compassion, charity and love. And we are all about to cease as a result."

"So Heart," Brain, Mind, and Ego replied together, "what is it you propose to do about it?"

"I want to tell you all this: Yes, I do indeed have charge of the central control system called the Brain. I am in constant communications with Spirit and I am the portal to Spirit. I reflect what is in the heart. However, I am tired and dying as you have all made me so. As you know, my duty is to inform the control center what chemistry it must launch into this human. I am the reflector of emotion and I have but one choice in sending the signal to the brain that will release the appropriate chemistry for the emotion. How many times must I repeat this issue? Your influence, neglect and action have forced emotional issues of conditional love, lack of compassion, confidence, inspiration, hope, despair, hate, envy, fear, jealousy, anger, and lack of generosity. That must be put right, regardless of what the Soul has planned for the human."

"That's judgment and big talk, Heart! And how do you propose to do that?"

"It is time to ask. I see none of you care to really represent the Soul. Ego cares not, Brain takes orders, and Mind sleeps and says things are ok. I am connected to the Soul as it is unconditional love as I am. That is its purpose and I am deeply coupled with my Chakra as the central point of balance with the human energy system and a direct connection to God. I simply ask that Soul, a part of God give us some truths. Then we shall see."

WHO CALLS ME ASKS THE SOUL?

"Where are you dear Soul?" asked the Heart.

"I, as always," responded the Soul, "am here listening to you all. I am always present to prod you and help you all evolve your destinies. All you have to do is ask of me and learn to listen. I, as a part of God, am designed to always provide you with truth. But understand that I can not force you to agree, it is only your choices that make your, and this human's reality"

"Are you reflected in the Higher Self?" asked the Heart.

"Yes, it is so, I as a Soul, am a tiny holographic part of God and all that is which you refer to as Consciousness. The Higher Self is what humans have constructed to represent the Spiritual side of me, also represented in the human subtle energy system of the upper three Chakras. These represent a higher Spiritual ability, connecting the physical body with Spirit. Many refer to this as the Higher Mind. The lower three chakras are referred to as the Lower Self, or the Lower Mind and is concerned with the more physical survival of the body. This is where the Ego has its duties."

"Are you saying that Ego is indeed doing its job properly?" asked the Heart.

"My dear Heart," replied the Soul, "there are certain things that you all must understand before the word proper is applied. There is a way that all that is, which includes all of you and the body you speak of, works within the natural laws of the Universe. When you understand this, then it is up to you to decide whether proper is an appropriate expression."

"So you are not judging what we do?" asked the Mind, Brain, Ego and Heart together.

"I, like God, do not judge. We only hope that you understand what you are, who you are, and that you have a wonderful life. We only hope that you make the choices to remember what you are and what your purpose is."

"Are you suggesting that we are eternal and part of God?" asked the Heart.

"Yes," replied the Soul, "but that is a very small part of it. I am part of God, and I am an integral component of you. But what I must tell you is that all these truths I am about to give to you are in love, and you all already know inside. You have not bothered to look there or listen. I am part of you and all that exists. The truths that I reveal reflect the expression of yours *as above so below* are there in you simply waiting to be discovered. Yes, the truth is that you are me, a Soul and certain energies which are eternal. You must first learn about the Laws of Purpose. But first, you need to understand our relationships."

"Yes," replied, the Heart, "I am puzzled as to why we are here together. Can you explain this, Soul?"

"I can dear Ones," replied Soul. "You are here because you are in a final instant of time where the body ceases its life on the Earth. It is a time of great transition and you are all simply a segment of Consciousness within the great Consciousness of God."

"But we speak to each other as if we were in the body. Is it dead?" asked the Brain.

"No, dear Brain, you and the body are simply in that instant of your time where there is no time or physical reality as you have learned to understand it through your five senses. The body is simply suspended in this place, between heartbeats. It can cease to beat, which will end its physical life, or it can continue to beat and live further."

"And what will decide either way?" asked Mind.

"You my dear Ones will," said Soul, "should you decide to not have the next beat, I will depart back to what I am which is a part of God. Should you decide otherwise, the heart will continue its beat and life in the physical form shall continue."

"I do not understand how," questioned Brain.

"Dear Brain," replied Soul, "we are all communicating telepathically within a medium of energy in a timeless domain of eternity. We are in my Consciousness in a vibratory level higher than you are used to. We are within what you have come to describe as the aura, an energy system around the physical body. This aura is me, the outer Soul containing three layers like your onions called etheric, astral and light bodies. We are all now communicating telepathically at a new, higher level of conscious perception."

"But, Soul," asked Mind, "are we still in the body?"

"Yes, dear Mind, we are all in and around it as it lies there, communicating through the aura, through our energy counterparts."

"Can you please explain?"' asked the Brain.

"Yes, dear Brain, I know this is hard for you to understand. The etheric is also the memory body, where true healing can happen, having long lasting affects on the physical body. It surrounds the body containing all the energy signatures that I connect with to provide the spark of life. You can support this etheric body by engaging in positive, soothing activities according to our Laws. Each of you have an energy counterpart or pair which resides here. All memory, senses, thoughts and experiences are here. So for example, you dear Brain, like Heart, Ego, and Mind have a higher vibration counterpart within this Consciousness, as I do."

"Soul, you mentioned layers," asked Ego, "what are they?"

"Dear Ego, around the etheric body is the astral body which means light or star. It is the outer soul, which is part of the much larger Consciousness. It is the first and last body to receive and send communications to God. It is the astral field which separates upon sleep or lost Consciousness. Death occurs when the astral connection is broken and I cannot return to the etheric body. As this body lying here has become weakened, the astral cord which connects me has weakened and the body may become unconscious."

"Are we, Soul, about to do that?" asked the Heart.

"Dear Heart, it is not mine or God's choice. It is all of you that will decide, or if there is no resolution, then the body will take its present course and not create another heartbeat. I am hopeful that to help me complete my ultimate purpose, you must all vibrate at a higher frequency so that you become closer to the vibration of God."

"Soul," asked the Mind, "how and when do we make such choices? It seems to be too late and we cannot agree."

"Dear Mind, and all of you. You may make such a choice after God and I have informed you of what you need to know about what choices exist. You do not appear to know the Purpose and Process of certain laws that have an affect on you all."

"Are you to reveal these to us?" asked Brain.

"Yes, if you wish to listen. It is your choice. But before we decide, you must know that the third field is the spiritual field. The spiritual field envelopes the entire astral field. It is the spiritual field that helps create the outer soul and is the Great Consciousness of God, and all that is. We shall speak of this again later. But first, do you wish to know about the Laws of the Universe and how they work with regards to humans?"

"Yes, please do tell us, Soul," all replied anxiously.

AND IS GOD PRESENT?

"Greetings to you all my loved Ones," echoed God through the ether. I am all that is and you are part of me. I am so pleased to be able to communicate so directly with you even though it is a crucial instant for the dear human body."

"We are listening," said everyone in great surprise.

"Loved Ones, you have summoned me of your own accord and I know what you feel and think as there are no secrets in this field of truth. Although you all know what Soul and I are to tell you, as it already is deep within you, it has not been called upon. As it is so, we are here to tell you about the Laws of Purpose and the Laws of Process. I wish to first bring into your Consciousness two Laws of Purpose."

"We are ready," replied all.

"Loved Ones, let me tell you about a law which I am going to refer to as the *Law of Ascension*. Soul here as part of Me has been on a mission to incarnate into this body. As it has informed you, it resides in the aura which surrounds and vitalizes the body. Yes, I hear you my dear Brain. You wonder why this is so."

"Let me continue, loved Ones. Humans are all here on this planet to evolve Consciousness until they become One with the light which created them which is Me. As part of God they are here to see the glory of all that is and remember who they are. All that exists is energy in a state of vibration so evolving Consciousness is synonymous with the process of raising vibrations. The purpose is to remember we are all a finite part of an infinite God by learning from experiences. When vibrations rise, this process allows people to remember their true lineage and the connection to the higher power of God which we are all a part of."

"So," said the Brain, "the body is the direct bridge to the physical, material world. Our personal Spirit is the direct bridge to the larger Universal Spirit. And the Mind is the direct bridge between body and Spirit?"

"Yes, Brain, and as you have discussed, there are three main components to the mind, namely the Higher Self (Spirit), the Lower Self (Ego) and the body's individual mind which bridges the other two."

"Is part of this design the chakras?" asked the Heart.

"Yes, my dear Heart, it is so. Humans are designed with energy centers called chakras that control the body's subtle energy fields. These invisible centers vibrate in unison with the body's surrounding subtle electromagnetic fields, communicating between universal energies and body functions just like in the field of acupuncture. Each center has specific purposes and capabilities. The higher top three chakras have Spiritual capabilities that cannot be activated or their true properties deployed until a human rises to a certain vibratory level as fueled by a specific energy force through ascension. The strongest positive energy forces that do this are love and compassion. The energy forces that stop the process are fear based. Once higher energy centers are activated as ascension progresses the human becomes *'enlightened'*, ultimately changing to a spiritual light being from where it came. As ascension progresses, new

Spiritual abilities become real when the upper chakras open."

"You mean like mental projection, psychic/distance healing, clairvoyance, clairaudience, clairsentience, precognition, telepathy, channeling, telekinesis, psychommetry, bilocation, levitation, time travel, teleportation, and so on?"

"Yes, my dear Brain," answered God.

"This set of new abilities and capabilities expands with the ascension process until you reach the ultimate vibratory state of pure spiritual energy, back into the etheric form where you are now."

"So bodies need to grow and be nourished to develop properly, as does our Spirit need to grow and develop. The link between the two, the Mind, has this responsibility of learning to ascend. Is that true?" asked the Heart.

"Yes, that is good," said God. "Now the second law you must be aware of is the *Law of Love*. It is coupled tightly to the Law of Ascension as the energy force of love is the vibrational energy engine, the true energy power in the Universe. It is God that is in the Heart. It is the Universal energy force upon which all life's purpose was designed. Unconditional love, when charged emotionally by a human, is a highly potent energy force recognized by God because it is the essence of God. Thus, the more love a human can generate, the more it synchronizes with the energy of the Universe, and the higher become its vibrations. The force of love harmonizes and creates coherent energy waves feeding the ascension stages, as do other love based emotions. I have heard you all discussing this."

"And," the Heart thundered, "the opposite negative, dark emotions based on fear and anger are energy disruptors that stop the ascension engine and descends the vibrations."

"Correct, my dear Heart," boomed God's thought. "As we choose love and compassion over fear or hatred to convert our life dramas into a personal experience, we raise vibrational thresholds, Consciousness, and contribute to a larger cosmic Consciousness, lifting the vibrations of the planet. The love and compassion environment make the planet a better place to live, reap abundance, joy and prosperity. As we open up to new abilities that are synchronized with these higher vibrations, we are able to co-create desires faster and evolve towards our Divine nature, leaving the importance of the material world behind. Our Divine nature, ability to give unconditional love, and reap peace, joy and abundance is our birthright towards our higher purpose. Do you all understand that?" asked God.

"Yes," everyone responded sheepishly.

"Mind," thought God, "I hear you need to know why this is so. Why has God broken apart into little pieces of Souls to do this, correct?"

"Yes, God, may I ask such a question?"

"Of course you can." God's thoughts penetrated, "as you lift your vibrations, all of me, because we are One, will come to your Consciousness, but in the meantime, I will tell you. God's Universe is founded on love. It is the natural force of all that exists. However, in order, to experience how wonderful it is, a vessel had to be created to feel the wonderful emotion of love. It is why Soul here, as a part of me volunteered to do this so I and many other parts of me could feel the wonder of it. The human body is such a vehicle and a contract was created as Soul's ultimate purpose to complete in human form. But the human had to be unknowing of the arrangement because otherwise it would realize it was God and it was all senseless. Thus, the chore was to find your ways through the dramas of life to remember who you were and regain the connection with Me – and go Home, as we call it."

"So, once we realize who we are and attain the ultimate purpose, we cease to need a body. Then we have ascended?" asked the Heart.

"As is the case when the body dies," replied God. "Now loved Ones, I hear many, many questions from you all. It is time for our dear Soul to tell you about the Laws of Process. These will answer many of your questions while I listen quietly. Remember that I hear all your thoughts."

AND SOUL SHALL EXPLAIN

"Now dear Ones," said the Soul, "it is time to speak of the Laws of Process. These are the laws which revolve around the Laws of Purpose. These are the way things work with regards to the human existence. Are we ready to hear these?"

"Yes," All replied.

"These are already known to you as they are part of the aura, so I am telling you nothing new. However, I must help you to bring it forward into your Consciousness. Normally, these would become your intuitive truths within your local Consciousness. They would of course become your reality as you raised vibrations to a second level of Consciousness, where you are now – partially – as I will demonstrate to you later. The third level of Consciousness occurs as you link directly with your external Soul and Light Body where you are then vibrating at the level of God's Mind, or Universal Consciousness and simply know all that is. You would know, and be God."

"Now, as you all seem to be quiet and perplexed dear Ones, I shall continue. There is another law of God which is best described as the *Law of Cosmic Intelligence.*"

"Is this the way God thinks?" asked the Mind.

"In a way, but it is more appropriate that it is the way things work reflecting back to us. It is a cosmic intelligence that exists everywhere and has an intelligent response system. It is within us and outside of us throughout the total Universe. It is the Divine whole that we all are part of. It is the medium of love or God, the other 90% of the

Brain. It is the DNA that is undeveloped that connects with that living medium. That living, conscious, intelligent medium is what keeps what we believe to have form and life functioning, spinning, moving and alive. It is that third level of Consciousness I just mentioned."

"But, Soul, how does this all work together, with the human body?" asked the Heart.

"My dear Heart, be aware that I, like the Mind here, and the Ego, are part of a Universal Mind, Consciousness and intelligence which holds the Akasic record of all that was or is. The Mind is not part of the physical body and resides in the local aura, which in turn links with the Universal Consciousness. The Universal Mind responds to emotion in a holographic way in that each piece is a mirror of the whole. A change in one piece mirrors through the whole. That is the way it is designed. In this way, the local Mind, or a small segment of local Consciousness holding all beliefs, thoughts, emotions and experiences, is reflected in the Universal Mind."

"Are you saying that a mirror of our combined local and global Consciousness, and our individual lives are a reflection of the local Consciousness like beliefs, energies and actions?" asked the Mind. "And is the global and planetary Consciousness a result of composite beliefs, energies and actions?"

"Yes," replied Soul, "at the minute level, DNA in the human is an integral part of the Universal holographic Mind being its connection to the rest of the Universal Mind and to Spirit. In a holographic sense, DNA is what makes a human and a human is like the DNA particle of God."

"Soul, I have a question for you," said the Ego. "What is karma all about? Does the human not have to work off bad energy that it agrees to?"

"Dear Ego, I understand why you ask such a question. What you are referring to is the *Law of Lesson*, or Karma. I must tell you that it has nothing to do with punishment, judgment or paying for mistakes. Karma is a natural law as there is no bad or good – all karma is neutral. Karma simply represents any situation that just happens to a human and no one, especially God does it to them. What the human chooses to attach to the situation that makes it as bad or good is a result of its own perception."

"Soul, are you saying that the bad energy Ego creates is fine?" asked the perplexed Heart.

"My dear Heart, good or bad is a perception. It can be perceived as a lesson from which you learn. Karma is simply a process of cause and effect – like a reflection. Now as I will elaborate on later, every action generates a force of energy that returns to the human in like kind."

"Do you mean the notions like *'what you sow you will reap'*, *'paying till the last penny'*, and *'what goes around comes around'?*" asked the Brain.

"Yes, my dear Brain, it is so. These are all expressions of how karma works and what the human chooses to reflect back as what it has learned from any event, experience or any situation."

"This is where the contract comes in, does it not?" asked the Ego.

"Yes, my dear Ego. Everyone has a '*contract*' of karma which unfolds on the planet as life's dramas – like the University of Life. The Law of Lesson is simply that the Mind and Soul have combined into a state linking with a physical form to experience karma – any and all situations – that we learn from. And those lessons, plus what we learn from them – which we alone perceive as having bad or good qualities – provide us with the University of Life through which I and you can evolve."

"So, if I understand this correctly," queried the Heart, "the result is that vibrations rise if we reflect back positive energy and we ascend, or we stay the same or lower vibrations if we reflect back negative energy – it is simply our choice. There is no judgment on this and of course the ultimate goal is to graduate from the University of Life fully ascended, remembering who we are as a finite part of an infinite Force we call God, having a life full of love and joy, being of service to all of humanity by working towards the higher good."

"Precisely. Well said, my dear Heart. God and Soul do not judge. It is you that judge yourselves by the Laws you impose. If you did not graduate the first time, I simply try again in another incarnation. Remember that Karma can only be balanced off in the physical body on earth, because God, through you and I must use the body to feel the emotions of life to achieve my higher purpose."

"So," the Mind asked, "you cannot control the body or me directly. It is the human, through me in a conscious state that can only make those choices?"

"True indeed, my dear Mind, and before we incarnate, I set up the situation called the contract that I need so that I can go into it again and do it differently to advance my ultimate purpose. The

Karma is something that I complete before I can complete my ultimate purpose and '*Go Home'* back to God."

"And," asked the Heart, "anger and depression is a condition of the physical body that prevents the Soul from completing its karmic contract?"

"Yes, I may have tried many ways to communicate and reach you all and the body, but if you refuse to listen, I am left with an unfulfilled contract."

"And that is not a big deal to you, to have failed in your contract?" asked the Ego.

"Not at all, Karma disappears as we convert bad to good. The more developed or advanced I am the more I tend to volunteer for more difficult tasks on earth in the next incarnation. It is not wrong or right as there is no judgment."

"Soul, are you saying that the body is expendable?" asked the Heart.

"It is so, my dear Heart. I may have undertaken an ultimate purpose, living a life of helping humanity progress, often at a cost to the physical self."

"Soul, that seems a bit selfish, like the Ego here. You both don't seem to care about the body."

"My dear Heart, you need to understand that you in particular, are made of two important pieces of energy. One is the dense physical part, the other and main part is lighter energy surrounding the dense part. Remember, the aura is the lighter part that is the connection with me and God and it is eternal."

"You mean," pondered the Brain, "it is like we are wearing a costume in a play at this University of Life playing out the show. When it ends, we take another costume and remember all we learned?"

"Yes, my dear Brain. It is so. It is recorded but not available to you in the next incarnation unless you have raised vibrations beyond a threshold, like you are in now."

"But the body, Heart, Brain all disappear and the Mind, Ego, and Energy systems remain?"

"The Ego is only a necessary function of the physical. As the human ascends, the need for Ego falls away. It is simply embedded in the Consciousness forever without any need for dense physical things."

"Soul," asked the Heart, "I am having some difficulty understanding why the body is expendable and it is not an issue what happens to it. Can you please elaborate?"

"My dear Heart, I understand your concern because you want the human to have a wonderful life of love, compassion and free of fear. I must tell you more about the other laws, such as the Law of Manifestation."

"Soul, do you mean the process whereby a human can bring something from invisible non-reality – like a thought, idea, or vision – into a visible state which it perceives to be real?" asked the Brain.

"Yes, my dear Brain, the process is one of converting energy into a different form through intent and actions. As everything is made of vibrating energy, this process behaves according to particular unique natural laws encompassing energy movement and minute subtle lines of force. Of particular importance here is how the energy is created and further energized by a human body. These energies are thoughts, emotion, words, objects, pictures, visualizations, and other such things that are part of the human communication systems. They all vibrate at their own specific frequencies and have unique characteristics – a unique energy signature so to speak. These energies operate under a sub-law of reflection and attraction where any energy signature created is reflected back by the Universal Intelligence."

"I understand clearly," said the Heart, "it thus appears to attract similar energy which is then reflected back to the source. The energy forms into packets. Once created and projected, through attraction, they seek out other packets in the form of events, people, thoughts, ideas and so on that will contribute to the manifestation of what the particular energy represents."

"Yes, my dear Heart, it is so. The Universal Intelligence will simply mirror back or reflect as best it can what the signature of the packet reflects. As a result, what the Mind *'thinks about, it brings about'* and *'energy flows where attention goes'* are things that the Mind and the Ego should *always* be aware of. The human energy machine is designed to always be manifesting energy packets and the energy creation process does not care whether it is dark (bad) or light (good) energy. This process is happening automatically whether you know it or not."

"I suspected that," acknowledged the Heart, "if someone does not pay attention, the machinery goes to autopilot unless someone decides to take the controls and pilot the process."

"Yes, the other point is no one of you has any idea when this will attract or manifest the results as there is a time lag between the energy initiation and when it reflects back. But the Universal Mind will nevertheless work towards finding the appropriate energies to give the desired experience. The speed of the manifestation process depends on the strength of the energy and clarity of the focus you place on the packet. It may take a lifetime or several lifetimes to achieve the desired signature depending on the complexity and strength of the energy. Or it may be a short time lag if the energy is highly focused and energized."

"Well, what I am hearing," said the Heart, "is the crucial process here is to learn to visualize and emotionalize in one world, then manifest the experience we want in the other 3D world. This is why you need to be acutely aware that '*what the Mind visualizes is what it materializes'*."

"Yes, my dear Heart. You must all be aware that the two most powerful energies are love and fear, characteristics that the human alone attaches to the packet. These two energies, depending on the strength, shorten the time lag and in worst case scenarios it can rapidly manifest *worst fears* or *greatest desires*."

"But that is what I have been saying about the Ego," stated the Heart, "it is always creating these fears and negative emotions that I then have to project to the Brain. At the same time I am sending signatures out with these terrible thoughts from the Mind that go and find more of the same. Oh, woe is me. This is worse than I thought."

"Well, my dear Heart, you must understand that the human, in conjunction with the Mind, made the choice to create that type of energy. Did they not?

Regardless of what Ego was saying, was there not a choice? Of course it is critical how letters, words, sentences, and thoughts are used. And it is true that these energies are projected at varying strength, carrying qualities that are further energized by human emotion. But how was the decision reached to choose the negative emotion that you are concerned about?"

"But, as I see it," responded the Heart, "a significant effect on the power of the energy is the level of emotion attached to the words. And when an energy packet is created by the Mind involving a word, thought, statement, object, or visualization for example, the human body becomes an energy enhancer activated through the Mind that adds qualities to the packet. I am feeding this process. I am very upset."

"Yes, dear Heart, what you say is true. But any word or thought has to be energized from neutral so it can have spin (negative/positive or dark/light), polarity (Yin/Yang or female/male) and intensity (strength of emotion) added to the energy packet before it is projected out to seek out its goal. But remember the true mission. The true mission of the Higher Self part of the Mind is to represent me to evolve the body towards the purpose of God. This, you now know is done by putting a positive spin on energy, balancing the polarity and adding genuine strong positive love based emotion."

"But Soul, this is what I am all fussed about. You are not being represented by Mind. It has been sleeping and Ego has a free hand at running the Brain, me and the human. It has become apparent that the focus of our awareness becomes the reality of our world. We manifest things in this world by starting with *thinking* about something, creating the *intent* to carry something out, *attracting* or seeking out the components to accomplish something and taking *action* to *manifest* it. I knew this but never correlated it with everyday thoughts. This process is being carried out automatically through these laws, or it can be accelerated by being cognizant of how to manifest or co-create proactively. I now know the key to proactive manifestation – taking control off autopilot is to use the universal language of word meaning and emotion intensifying the energy created. That created energy best manifests a desire when it is created by feeling the end result – what you want to manifest. But how can I do that when Ego is playing and Mind is sleeping?"

"My dear Heart, you must now clearly understand the *Law of Free Will*. Everything the human experiences has a choice associated with it. The interpretation or perception brought about by experiencing any event, and the action taken through intent is a choice that is the human's alone. The Mind is what the human uses to do that, is it not? It can choose to ignore Ego as it chooses to ignore me. The experience it has with regards to any event, and the personal feelings, thoughts and reactions created are a choice. The energy packets are assigned characteristics created by all of you. More pertinent is that the Mind, you and Ego can choose love based emotional energies or fear based emotional energies. Any subsequent intent to act from that choice, and the act itself - a direct manifestation of the intent - is clearly all yours. The emotions surrounding the choices come from your body through your Mind. It is possible for someone or some thing to restrict your body from a free choice, but it is impossible for anything else but you to force your Mind into a choice. That is free will and is a Universal Law."

"Ok, Soul, are you saying the Mind is the one that must make the choice to the good side?"

"I am saying dear Heart that the Mind has the choice to make that decision."

"Then it is the Mind that is not doing its job and should be fired. Why is the Mind not filtering and representing you? I know what damage is being done. The Ego doesn't really care and the Brain only takes orders. The power words and resulting emotions should revolve around love, joy, harmony, reverence, compassion, forgiveness, gratitude and charity. These *harmonize* with your purpose of ascension and work toward reflecting more of the same back to the human. What I have been saying is that things are amplified even further with good feelings *coming from the heart.* They immediately dissolve negative energy and keep focused on accelerating the ascension track. I think this philosophy eventually creates a snowball effect of good positive energy attracting more positive energy. But what good is my thinking if the Mind sleeps and doesn't care?"

"Dear Heart, like the Law of Free Will, I cannot dictate what is right or wrong and I cannot tell you how to run things. That is the Law. Right? If you all decide to pay attention to these laws and ascend, then yes, the Mind is an integral part of making it happen. If not then there is no judgment, but it is of course my wish that you all begin to realize your functions and work together towards your ultimate purpose."

"Well, Soul, the way I see this is the Ego should rule the lower three chakras, and I rule the upper three and it takes orders from me and the Mind is there to consider you and me as its consultants."

"But, my dear Heart, have you considered the Chakras? They also have input and they in the best state need to be balanced. Much of the problems with both the Spirit and physical dysfunction you speak of resides in how well these are balanced between negative and positive."

"Oh my," whimpered Heart, "I am thinking this is all hopeless, Soul. Ego does not care, Brain takes orders, I am being abused, you can't step in, Mind sits there thinking all is well and sleeps, and now you say someone has to balance the chakras. Who?"

"You, my dear Heart, you!"

"Me." said the Heart totally stunned.

"Dear Heart, and all of you, let me complete my truths before we discuss this. For now, yes, the Heart is the balance center and I am not in the formula because I do not judge right or wrong, and I love you all. I will not conflict, judge, or raise concerns. I can only nudge you and suggest a good course of action but you must all listen."

"I believe I speak for all, Soul when I say we will listen to you now," said the Mind.

"Then dear Ones, let me tell you of the *Law of Intent*, or action. Something has to instigate an action of giving energy life. Intent is a highly potent subtle force that triggers an action. Intent brings about a specific action deployed by you. Much of the energy the human produces comes from an automatic reaction whereby some emotion is attached to it is not what was intended. So suddenly when an event triggers a reaction, Heart, Brain, Ego or Mind can react in fear or anger automatically thereby attaching an emotion, quality thoughts or word. Then the *Law of Manifestation* works to return like energy. But you can all deploy intent proactively by controlling how to react, or by purposely triggering intent to do something of different choice."

"Yes, I understand that," replied the Heart.

"And in addition, the most powerful means of manifesting is to create energy packets with strong, true feelings that are without hidden motive, judgment, or desire with attachment. Because of our purpose and design, the most powerful feelings are love, compassion, forgiveness, gratitude, charity and tolerance because they are in harmony with the prime purpose and its force, adding power to the energy packet."

"I have learned," confirmed the Heart, "that fear and anger are strong emotions which are the universal language understood by all including God. It is clear that '*what one resists persists*'. Producing the opposite of what is desired. And it matters not that the world is negative. We must all work to change that perception."

"Well said, dear Heart, now let us go to the *Law of Perception*. Reality to the human is simply decided through the body's five-sensory system as interpreted by Brain. Yet, this is a narrow spectrum of all that is. It is here that the Brain and Mind have created the concept of linear time within which material things appear solid. They are not. As you pass this perception, you will all see 95% is intelligent space. You are in this space now. It is the total Consciousness of God. If a human has a dream there is no material or time there. It is simply un-manifested energy. Visualization is a product of the Mind. It, through the Mind, is the link to the inner dream world and is also energy. The Mind is the crossover means between the inner dream world and the outer real world. To Brain, as you have noted, which is partially controlled by all of you, there is no clear distinction as to whether images, visualization, dreams or what is seen in a conscious state are real or not. Yet either can affect the body and its emotions. These are simply energy and all the same to the Brain. The process of visualization is a fundamental component of making any perception into reality. The common thread that connects you to the invisible spiritually evolved world is imagination and intent, particularly to ascend. This is how working with visualization will create reality. This is how the Mind can make a dream come true. On truth, it is the Mind and the Heart that can choose a highest point of perception, and make it a reality."

"Yes," replied the Mind and the Heart, "we can see this now."

"Good, dear Ones. Now let me explain the *Law of Connection or Grace.* It has to do with a direct connection channel to Me and God. There are special intents, actions, words and emotions that I and God are warmed to in our Hearts and respond directly to. These are prayers as well as forgiveness, meditation, and blessing. By using these direct connectors, the human is able to accelerate ascension, and its manifestation ability referred to as co-creation. Certain words and the type of emotional energy they carry are in strict harmony with our prime purpose of Love and Ascension. They carry a strong synchronization making a direct connection to the Divine. Forgiveness, synonymous with the process of '*blessing'* is such a word. If a human wants to change something they must forgive the party that created the guilt, hate, anxiety, or whatever is bothering it. It is strong energy medicine when genuine emotion is attached – from the Heart."

"Understood." said Heart.

"Yes, dear Heart, prayer is also a direct channel as is meditation. Prayer has four components, regardless of race, or religion. These are the *acknowledgement* (our Father in Heaven), *faith* (give us this day our daily bread), *gratitude* (Thank you for…), and a *close* (Amen) which means '*So be it',* or '*Let it be'.* In other words, what is asked for in the faith section is *done – thank you*. The feeling of being done is synonymous with faith – something is already accomplished. Through your faith and belief, you acknowledge power in creation as co-creators. So when you speak directly to God, every thought is treated like a prayer and every prayer is answered. It goes beyond judgment, ready to talk to the Universal Intelligence. The words and thoughts come from a deeper place if they carry genuine positive emotion with them. This is the path to miracles and modifying DNA which is all part of the Universal Mind. The stronger the emotion associated with the faith, the faster things happen."

"I am also clear, Soul, that meditation is another direct conduit isn't it?" asked the Mind.

"Yes, dear Mind, it is so. Meditation is the means to go within to truth and peace, getting in touch with the real you and me. In lowering Brain's waves this way, Mind can neutralize the outer world and move into the inner world. This is where direct communications to me and God becomes the purpose. I can then enter local Consciousness where a link to all that is known and is, can be made. In this place, there is no clock time and within it is the world of dreams, feelings, and imagination where Mind can enter a boundless realm of possibilities to experience by simply being within it."

"We understand," everyone said together.

"Now we must talk about the final *Law of Coherence*. It has to do with balancing everything. We briefly talked about there being a balance point in the chakra system. We shall talk more about this later. If balance between the spiritual and physical worlds does not happen then psychological and physiological dysfunctions in the body occur. It is your duty to create balance. There are many invisible subtle energies that balance the human body. These are blocked by negative thought and emotions. As the Heart is the source of emotion, courage and wisdom, it is therefore the balancing point. It must work to keep everything in *balance* – coherent – so a body can function in an optimal fashion. When the Law of Coherence is violated, dysfunction and imbalance are a result where various diseases are free to flourish, as you have all noted."

"So Soul," asked Mind, "we should always be working to balance the Ego with Heart and Soul. And the Heart must work towards balancing the chakra energy systems with God?"

"You are partially correct dear Mind. You must all bring life's purpose forward and decide that the Laws of Purpose and Process are your faith and belief. In this way you can all bring this forward into your local Consciousness."

"I have a question, Soul," asked Ego. "You favor your purpose and Gods Laws that you have placed before us. Yet you say there is no judgment, right or wrong regardless of what path is chosen albeit destructive or constructive – love or fear. If such is the case, why should any one of us care?"

"Dear Ego, that is a valuable question. In truth, you are stating the truth. It is a matter of choice, intent and perception, such is true. But what is important is that you know the truth, and have an awareness of who and what you are. How that truth is used in the lifetime is indeed yours to deploy. My objective is to simply provide you all with a different option which can provide a path to abundance, peace, joy, and love in a different way than you have been pursuing. And of course, through ascension, and raising vibrations there is a much different life available than you currently grasp. But yes, dear One, these are your choices."

"I see," replied the Ego.

THE CHAKRA CHILDREN SPEAK

"Dear ones," said the Soul, "we are not yet done with balancing energies. There are many energy systems in the body besides you. I want you to meet some of my favorites of which there are seven. They are like playful children and they can be easily deceived."

"Soul, do you speak of the chakras?" asked the Heart.

"Yes, you see," replied the Soul, "you all have an energy counterpart that exists as part of the whole. You know now it resides in the aura so it can interface between your physical human and my Spiritual body. You are all either a direct part of the whole, resident in the body or you have a physical part resident in the body which has certain duties to perform, just as you do, dear Heart."

"You speak of the Heart chakra?" queried the Heart.

"Yes, and you my dear Heart are the balance point of all chakras. As you all have aptly noted, there are three below you which are focused on worldly aspects that Ego is concerned about, and the three above are Spiritually focused that I am more concerned about. But please don't get me wrong, I am concerned about how they all relate to both the physical and Spiritual worlds. Should they not be balanced, I feel compassion for the human as it can result in undue hardships."

"I understand that," replied the Heart. "but how do these interrelate?"

"I shall tell you," replied the Soul, "again, there are seven main energy centers within the body. They are my entry and exit points for the communication between the DNA in every cell and God. These create an invisible system of subtle energy centers sensitive to energies both inside and outside of the body that project backward and forward from the center vertical axis of the body."

"Such as the Heart chakra," confirmed the Heart.

"Yes dear One. These chakras connect critical body organs and their functions through onion-like layers of bodies to God and the life force. If they die, as in your case, dear Heart, the area of responsibility ceases to function and the body will die as the true energy center, the life force, has left for Home."

"Soul," Brain asked, "as long as the connection to God, and you as part of God, exists, so does the human body?"

"Yes, dear Brain, you are partially correct. There are very critical centers like you and the Heart, and there are less critical centers that can fall into imbalance. But nevertheless, they perceive sensory energies and transmit impulses to vital organs in their vicinity of the body that in turn control the endocrine system. They regulate many, many different body functions through the production of hormones that are released into the bloodstream. You all understand that human psychological and physiological functions are controlled and influenced this way. They all vibrate at specific frequencies and connect with the other bodies to create a bio-electromagnetic energy system that keeps the body alive and well."

"Such as when you leave the body, the life force is gone and the body dies?" asked the Mind.

"Yes, my dear Mind. Now, it is time to meet these children of mine. I would first like to introduce Root. Yes it is a funny name!"

"Greetings All, I am Root, the first or base chakra located at the base of the spine. I am closely linked with the adrenal glands as well as other organs in my region. My primary function is survival as I ground the body and connect it with Mother Earth. If I am not strongly grounded then Mind and Body will find it very difficult to enjoy life. My energy gives the physical will of being and the will to live. When the energies are balanced it allows the body to nourish and look after itself with care, love, discernment and sensitivity. When I am balanced, the human has assertiveness, courage, strength of will, and pioneering tendencies."

"Root," asked the Brain," what does it mean to be balanced?"

"I, like all others of my chakra family, provide the communication to the DNA of the cells from my region downward. I work with the adrenal system in the human. When I feel good, I am balanced. I work in harmony with my opposite, Crown whom you will meet. The balance must be between the Spiritual part above with the physical part below. Otherwise the total well-being of the human is compromised and falls to dysfunction."

"And when imbalance occurs?" asked the Brain.

"Too much energy into me often results in too much negative control, greed, and selfishness. There may be sexual issues and behavior seeking thrills through drugs, alcohol, sex, and addictions.

There may also be an inability to let go of things. This desire to maintain control and possession can result in being overweight, with a reluctance to exercise, and result in a withdrawing from nature. Rage, anger and violence can be typical defense mechanisms as behind these actions is always a fear of losing something that provides security, well-being, and the basics of survival. This leads the human to enjoy playing the victim throughout life, creating insecurity, self-pity, aggression, and fear."

"Thank you dear Root. Now let us hear from dear Sacral."

"Greetings All, I am Sacral, the center of relationship. I am located just below the navel in the human and I deal directly with the lower intestine, kidneys, and reproductive organs. I deal with the spleen in men and the uterus in women. My primary function deals with the human relationship to everything outside which includes the ability to connect with other humans, the Universe, the Earth, Nature, and Animals – all that is. I have a lot to do with sensuality of touch and the innocent desire for pleasure, being nonjudgmental, and having spontaneous enjoyment so I affect how well humans can love each other. When I am balanced with Brow, whom you will meet, and feeling great, it allows the human to give off a very positive energy field. It would be very sanguine and have a great sense of well being. It would allow the joy that comes from liking the self and loving life. The result is a healthy, balanced appetite for life without being over-indulgent. When I am in an ideal state, the human will feel alive, confident and happy, experiencing and expressing a measure of personal power, accepting itself and having a love of self without Ego. The clearer this is, the more the human can see the truth of any situation, including the manipulative behavior of others. It will know its own power and will be self-confident."

"And when you are not feeling well?" asked the Brain.

"If I am not well, the human will tend to become a martyr, become unhappy, relinquishing all responsibility for well-being, feel undeserving of fulfillment, dissipate energy by seeking approval from others, and therefore have no energy for itself. There will be a perception that there is never enough and life is full of suffering."

"Thank you dear Sacral," said Soul, "now may I introduce Solar."

"Greetings All, I am Solar, the center of personal power. I am the third chakra located in the center of the waist. I am closely connected to the organs of that region such as stomach, small intestine, liver, pancreas, and spleen, as well as the skin and nervous systems. I am closely tied to the immune system. I have two main functions. The first relates to how the human relates to itself, from which arises genuine self-worth, self-esteem, and self-confidence. The other function relates to being the seat of personal power. When I am feeling good and balanced the human is confident, alert, optimistic, and good humored. When I am working well with my twin, Throat, whom you will meet, the human has vitality, creativity and imagination."

"And when you are not balanced?" asked the Mind.

"If I am not in balance it causes self-doubt that creates a negative energy, working like a toxin within the body. It paralyzes and weakens the body, lowering energy making life very dreary. This stops the human from flourishing, it being full of doubt, less empowered and having little self-worth. This leads to looking for control of everything in order to feel powerful. The human will constantly be overwhelmed by emotion or find it difficult to express any emotion, with feelings of inferiority, being over analytical, sarcastic, and pessimistic."

"Thank you dear Solar. Now we must hear from Heart. But before we do, you must all know by now that Heart, whom you have been communicating with, is the physical aspect. The Heart we are to hear from next is the energy counterpart connected directly to God. We shall speak of this later."

"Greetings All, I am Heart the center of love. I am the fourth chakra located in the center of the chest. I stand alone and have no twin, no correspondence with any other chakra. This is because my communication is directly from God through the outer Soul as transmitted directly to me. I deal with the thymus, heart, blood system, lungs and other functions in my area. I am about perfect balance and love. When this is achieved, it leads to a perfect balance of bliss and enlightenment — balancing the other chakras below me and above me. I balance the spiritual and physical realms. When I am well, the human will empathize and sympathize, as well as perceive beauty in itself and others. It will exude a great passion for life, and take responsibility for how it feels. When I am well, the human is able to love everything and all people, animals, nature, the universe, and God. I am the center of compassion, generosity, harmony, balance, and loving."

"And," the Heart asked, "when you are not?"

"Dear Heart, I know that you know this. If I am unbalanced, the human will have a tendency to act one of two ways. One way is that it will tend to love too much, giving from the heart level and receiving very little love back, which creates an unhealthy imbalance in the physical. The second way is that the human may feel incapable of real intimacy and will resist feeling. It will act as if everything is fine and avoid the truth of its feelings. It will avoid bonding by creating conflicts, tension and drama and then use this as an excuse to distance itself. Love becomes a mental exercise, creating indifference, jealousy, miserly, and bitterness."

"Yes, Heart Chakra, I am aware of the results of that. We all see this body ravaged by fear and anxiety that have produced heart diseases, circulatory problems – because of its power seeking attitudes created by Ego."

"But Heart, we must be balanced ourselves first. We must be balanced with God, who we represent directly. No other Chakra has this direct Divine relationship."

"I see a new picture evolving here," responded Heart.

"Thank you, Dear Heart, now let us hear from Throat."

"Greetings All of you. I am Throat, the center of truth. I am the fifth chakra located in the throat. I have responsibilities in my area, dealing with thyroid and parathyroid glands and functions in my area such as neck, throat, and mouth. I am responsible for communications so I fulfill the function of self expression, and the ability to speak the truth. I also deal with willpower, which means I govern the will required for translating things into action. I am strengthened and enriched each time the human expresses truth and integrity, acting as a bridge centered in the Heart. When I am balanced with my pair, Solar, the human is trustworthy, reliable, sincere, interested, and true to self and others."

"And when you are not happy?" asked the Mind.

"If I am not happy, the human will hide its true self, sometimes silenced by shame, living in self-hurt. It will suppress its feelings, including love, hurt, frustration, and anger. Such will lead to depression, limited self-expression and being closed off. It will feel safer to hide in silence than to say anything, living a lie to protect itself, and often turn to abuse in order to numb the Spirit and Soul with food, alcohol, work, and drugs. This means being unfaithful, untrustworthy, self-righteous, and cold."

"Thank you my dear Throat, now let us hear from Brow."

"Greetings All, I am Brow, also known as the third eye chakra. I am the center of intuition, located in the center of the forehead just above the brows. I have responsibility over the pituitary gland. I open up higher mental powers, intelligent discernment, knowledge and mind power. I give the ability to understand non-physical things, and abstract concepts, also controlling the degree of higher capabilities. These would be intuition, clairvoyance, dreaming, out of body experiences, inner knowing and experiences in the spiritual realm of the Soul. When I am fully functioning and happy, a greater Consciousness abounds as the human becomes connected. The dream world is rich and meaningful and the invisible worlds are more available. The human develops a deep knowing, is wise and lives from the place of inner trust. The role in the greater picture of humanity becomes foremost in its Mind, working towards the ultimate purpose in life. The human will be highly intuitive, faithful, clear sighted, have high integrity, and have an orderly mind."

"And what if you are not happy?" asked the Mind.

"Then it gives rise to insanity, hysteria and panic attacks. If I am not fully functioning, most of the Mind's thoughts will be controlled by old, unresolved, emotional patterns which often come from the opinion of others and childhood issues. There will be an unbalanced development of the intellect, tending to theorize about everything. The human will not be dramatically in tune with what is going on and use control to avoid feeling. This will often be restrictive in the capacity to experience joy, being very opinionated and not trusting experiences, needing everything to be explained logically. The human will not trust intuition, have a scattered mind, be inconsiderate, and have blinkered vision."

"Thank you dear Brow, now we must listen to Crown."

"Greetings to you All. I am Crown, the center of Spirit. I am the seventh chakra located in the top of the head. I am connected to the whole of creation and am responsible for the pineal gland. I provide unity with God, the human Soul and ultimate purpose in life. I am connected to the conscious working of the Brain, making sense of raw information received from sense organs. I am responsible for memory and planning, giving insight and grounding, particularly when I am happy working with my pair Root. When I am pleased, the human becomes One with the whole universe and can experience a very high state of Consciousness. This helps it move between God and the body. I can then reveal to the human all of its Spiritual practices, meditations, prayers, devotions, and Spiritual needs. The external world will no longer feel particularly fulfilling. What may have given the body and Mind joy or contentment isn't there any more. The human, together with Mind, will not seek external power because it will know that the truth lies within and it has tapped into this limitless resource. This truth tells it to let go of anything that limits it. It reflects great intelligence, abundance, wisdom, radiance, beauty, creativity, and brilliance. The mind and body will show reverence for all life, be self-sacrificing in the service of others, and have the ability to see the appropriate route for the benefit of the Higher Self, and the Soul."

"And tell us what is the case if you are not happy," asked the Mind.

"Then the human will be easily deluded. It will feel like an orphan, feeling empty because there is always more that it needs and should be doing. It will experience an over-proud, narcissistic, ungrateful, and self-important resistance of Mind to a self-development attitude. Such negative aspects will include having no concern for others, feelings of superiority, and a lack of contact with reality. The Mind may even try to impose its will on everybody."

"Thank you dear Crown. Now we have a full picture of the major energy centers in a human. These wonderful children play a vital functional role relating to physiological functions with direct affects on psychological behaviors. Functioning as pumps or valves, they regulate the flow of energy through the body energy system, reflecting decisions the human makes concerning how it chooses to respond to conditions in its life. The valves change as it decides what to think, and what to feel, deciding this through a perceptual filter. In this way it has a choice as to how it experiences the world around it and affects the body."

"I see," said the Mind, "all of the body senses, perceptions, possible states of awareness, and everything it is possible for it to experience, can be divided into seven categories associated with a particular chakra. Thus, the chakras represent not only particular parts of the physical body, but also particular parts of Consciousness. Tension in Consciousness is felt by the chakra associated with that part of Consciousness experiencing the stress, level and length dictating the level of dysfunction."

"Yes, dear Mind," said the Soul, "now that you have all heard these wonderful children, you know that they function towards balance, but they do not have the ability to control the human's emotions that can affect balance. Has it occurred to any of you who can?"

"It is a choice of the Heart and the Mind," said the Brain. "They are the energy makers of emotion, thought that can alter the body."

"It is so," said Soul, "and how must it work if the human wants to attain the purpose of life?"

"They must work together as a team," answered the Brain.

NEW CONSCIOUSNESS AWAKENS

"Now, dear Ones, I would like to engage you in something else momentarily. Have you noticed how we communicate?"

"Yes," answered the Mind, "we are communicating telepathically without human speaking."

"Correct, my dear Mind. You are in the second level of Consciousness where part of me resides. Yet you are aware that a body with Brain and Heart are physically in the body and you, Ego and myself, along with my Chakra Children, are where?"

"We must be part of the aura, part of a Universal Mind of God which has no form only pure energy," replied Mind.

"My dear Mind, now that you are in a higher vibratory state of Consciousness, note how easy it becomes to perceive and manifest. Let us change your point of perception now. If you dare, look down at the body lying there on the bed. Can you see it?"

"Why, yes Soul, by simply thinking it, I have raised above it and see it as separate. Has it died?"

"No, but it could and then the result would be the same. Can you still feel and see, and communicate with Brain, Ego, and Heart?"

"We can," cried Brain, Heart, and Ego. "I sense them and we are telepathically connected."

"And yet all the senses, memory, and emotions belonging to the physical human are intact?"

"Yes," replied all, very bewildered.

"Can you see each other?" asked the Soul.

"Yes, we see each other as a field of energy, like a cloud which we are within," said Brain.

"Do you feel, or sense anything new from this position?"

"I sense emotion from Brain, Mind, Ego, and you," pondered the Heart, "I feel peace and wonderment, like there is much more to me. And I feel as we are One. I feel a strong emotional connection to you."

"As do we," echoed the Ego, Mind and Brain.

"You, dear Mind, have changed your point of perception and are connected with a larger Consciousness including me and God. Did you know you could do that at will? And Heart, did you know likewise?"

"Soul," the Heart pondered, "we have at the will of Mind, severed and become whole with God? And I can do the same?"

"Yes, my dear Heart, as can you all. It is this medium which connects directly and your purposes are clearly known. They are the same, and you are of One. Does that change your perception of what you must all do?"

"We..." All suddenly stuttered.

"Oh, loved Ones," God injected its thoughts and mind, "are you so surprised to see me now?"

"I see you, God, as an angelic white being of pure radiating energy exuding only love. I feel it so strongly like it was an indescribable peace and wholeness," cried Heart.

"And," God replied, "you see each other as well?"

"We see and feel each other," said the Mind with excitement.

"You have simply, separated the body's aura," said God, "as the outer Soul containing the etheric, astral and light bodies to the second level of Consciousness. You will now understand the etheric is also the memory body, where true healing can happen, to have long lasting affects on the physical body. You can support the etheric body by engaging in positive, soothing activities according to our Laws. This is done through ascension. It leads to the third level of Consciousness."

"We, are all intact, outside of the body!" exclaimed Brain, "this is truly incredible."

"My precious Brain," laughed God, "you are so funny rooted in your local conscious wisdom. Astral means light so you have simply entered the Consciousness of the true outer Soul. It is where you are part of Me. We are One Mind, One Consciousness and you are as eternal as Me."

"So," the Mind stated, "this is like when death occurs and the astral connection is broken. Soul cannot return and the spark of life is gone from the body. This body we belong to has become weakened, and the astral cord has weakened. Is this what occurs in a Near Death Experience as well?"

"Yes, my precious Mind, it is so," confirmed God, "a miracle has the same result of allowing the aura from local Consciousness to see, feel and connect with the Soul and Me."

"By this little exercise," shouted the Heart, "we have also done the equivalent of an Out of Body experience!"

"Yes, indeed," said the Soul, "it is a miracle which can also create life changing actions and perception in the human, just as a Near Death Experience has."

"Yet," said the Heart, "we are all One, including our Chakra children. And we can feel each other think and feel as if we were One."

"But my dear Ones, why should any of you be so surprised?" asked God," are you not One within one body?"

"It seems so," replied the Mind, "but while in the body we were separate, working at different functions of the whole. Now we can see each other in a different form, feel each other and know that our ultimate purpose is the same as we are all a part of God. This has been an unconscious part of all of us until now."

"But, dear Mind," said the Soul, "is it possible that none of you were listening to me? I am always prodding you with alternative thoughts from and about God. You all know what the purpose is and how the Universe works. You have simply chosen to ignore the call of intuition through which we speak to you as we speak now."

"Yes," the Mind said, "I have been asleep and have let Ego have his way. Heart is right about this. I must wake up and work as One by changing my perception to a higher place."

"Yes," the Brain said, "I have been protective about blame and sometimes despondent about what I must do to this body. I must wake up and work as One to create coherent energies."

"Yes," said the Ego, "I have been overzealous in my directives to Heart and Brain. I must understand that abundance, prosperity, and a good life can be created by the Laws of Manifestation and others that you have given us, and that it can be done without fear and anxiety placed upon the human."

"Yes," said the Heart, "I have been too critical of Ego, and Mind and must wake up to how directly connected I am to the Chakras and God. We must work together to go to a higher point of perception representing what I am and what our purpose is."

"Yes," said the Soul, "you are indeed all as One and you are loved by me and God. We are always around speaking quietly to you all."

"Yes," said the Chakra Children, "we have been too concerned about dysfunctions and must work with Heart to balance at the center of love."

"What I am hearing dear Ones," said God, "is that there is not a requirement to divide responsibilities and have a reporting hierarchy as that is a human construct. I am hearing that you are all like a well oiled Spiritual machine with moving parts that work as a partnership, without strife, conflict or fear."

"But God," queried the Mind, "as soon as we go back into the body, will we not tend towards forgetting this lesson again?"

"You may," responded the Soul, "but you can at will speak with Me and God. As you understand the Laws which we have told you about, you know now that the process of meditation, or prayer are ways in which you can also shift to the higher vibrations and communicate directly at higher levels of Consciousness. It is also very sound for the human to begin repair of its Earthly body by ascension and raising its vibrations to a lighter state, as guided by the Mind of course."

"And another point, dear Heart," said Soul, "is that you are also a brain with 65% of you being neural cells much like Brain. Once you open properly and are balanced, gain intuition and balanced emotion, integrating me and God with access to wisdom and an openness, you are the most powerful energy generating machinery in the body. You are indeed much stronger than Brain, and it is easier to connect with me. But you must all always remember that love heals all. Such is the way of all and it transcends all that exits."

"Yes," said Heart, "and I was quick to blame Brain, yet I am the guilty one as I can create signals of disharmony through emotion I create. Clearly, I must be cognizant of that and not react swiftly, working closely with Mind to bring a wider, more favorable conscious to the human."

"Well said, Heart," answered Soul. "you are a highly complex, self-organized information processing center with its own functional brain that communicates with and influences the cranial brain via the nervous system, hormonal system and other pathways. These influences profoundly affect brain function and most of the body's major organs, and ultimately determine the quality of life."

"But Soul, what is to happen to us now? We have seen God. We have seen you and we are detached from a body that lies between heartbeats. How is life to continue?" asked Mind.

"And, God," Ego asked, "what is to happen to me? What must I do now?"

"Please, please, my beloved Ones," answered God, "all you must remember is that you are part of me. You, with this human, are here to find and follow a passion and be true to your Heart. All you must do is simply use the will you all have and give intent to make choices involving your perceptions of reality. All you must do is understand that the Laws we have taught you are for you to reflect on and consider so you may be aware there is more to your Earthly life than you understand in your local Consciousness. All you must understand is that the path of ascension may give you a wonderful life and it can become grander and grander as you expand your levels of Consciousness. And it is all in your power to choose this path."

"God," asked Mind," "what will happen if we cannot agree, then what?"

"Well, loved One, you as the Mind know the answer to this question, especially now that you are out of the local Consciousness. I must ask you this; Do you know how you relate to Consciousness?"

"Consciousness", replied the Mind, "is that which is brought forward in thoughts, memory, and experiences that we perceive as our reality. I hold, and create these perceptions and thoughts when in a conscious state. In effect, I am Consciousness, or at least a part of it."

"And, dear Mind, may I ask, what about when you are in an unconscious state?"

"God, that appears to be like now. It is the other part. This Consciousness is much expanded and limitless. So I as Mind am a smaller segment of the whole. It must be likewise with the whole of God Consciousness. In my local Consciousness, I am not aware of the rest."

"But you are now," answered God, "is it not that your awareness has simply expanded into a larger Consciousness? And did you not say thoughts that you bring forward into your Consciousness are what become reality?"

"Yes. Thoughts become ideas, concepts, beliefs, actions and hence reality."

"But are you not the key generator of thoughts brought into that reality?"

"I am not sure, God. There are many thoughts that enter me that do not create a reality."

"Such as, may I ask," queried God.

"These are like dreams, imagination, feelings, and idle thoughts that may come to me."

"But perhaps these are worthy of your attention, not imagination and idle, such as what you are experiencing now. You would have deemed dreams and thoughts about this as idle, would you not have?"

"Yes, God, it is so."

"Let me ask you this, dear Mind, when Brain processes information that interprets physical situations from the body sensory system, and a thought is brought forward into Consciousness, do you have a chance to determine what is perceived from that thought?"

"Yes, I do," answered Mind, "I have a choice."

"And dear One, what if Ego," asked God, "who would like the human, and of course you, to initiate an action which may be harmful or destructive, do you have a chance to decide on the course of action on these thoughts?"

"Yes, I do," answered Mind, "I have a choice."

"And what if our dear Heart, or our dear little Chakras were sending a signal of discomfort, would that possibly become thoughts brought into Mind to act on?"

"God, I suddenly know the answer to that," cried the Mind, "it would all come to me as thoughts that have not yet become true Consciousness, like being part of the unconscious. They would be what I refer to as '*in the back of my Mind*' waiting to be a thought brought to the '*front of my Mind.*' I know that Soul must also communicate to me that way."

"And dear Heart, how do you communicate with Mind?"

"God," Heart responded, "I send signals to the Brain and Mind as imbalance and discomfort in the Heart."

"God," Brain continued, "I pick up discomfort and dis-ease in various regions of the body. These reflect imbalances which when converted to thoughts to the Mind are feeling of something not being proper, balanced or quite functional."

"Which, Dear Ones," said God, "eventually manifest into disease and dysfunction. Perhaps even death?"

"I am seeing a new picture," said the Mind, "the expressions such as *'gut feeling', 'knowing the truth', 'seeing with my third eye', 'from the heart', 'intuitive feeling'* are reflections of the chakras. These are communication pathways describing balance between upper and lower chakras."

"Yes, dear Mind," said God, "they will also signal discomfort and a not-at-peace feeling from their respective areas of the body. Soul, Heart and I are sensitive to these as we are connected. But our connection through the local Mind is not so clear. You see, my beloved Ones, you know now that your local Consciousness is wanting to evolve into its next level, and onto the greatest Consciousness of all – where we are Home and all One together. The link between us all is our dear Mind."

"And I have been asleep," mumbled Mind, "with much backlogged as thoughts in the back of my Mind, not listening to signals of despair, and letting all others take responsibilities."

"Dear Mind," comforted God, "do not be so harsh on yourself. I have heard all of you being harsh with yourselves, but there is no right or wrong or any judgment. You are the ones that judge. There are simply choices you all can make. We hope you will find and follow a passion through the vehicle of body. We hope you will find your path to ascension to enjoy the wonderful experiences which can be had by following your passions. We hope you use your will and intent to expand your Consciousness beyond where it is into a vast world of unending, eternal possibilities. And if you happen to burn out your body in following dreams and passions, that is just fine since you are eternal. But, if you prefer to do as you are doing now, and burn out your body now, that is fine as well. All we want you to know is who you are and that there are many other choices to experience great joy, love and passions."

"So, God, what happens now?" asked Mind.

"My beloved Mind, now I can answer Heart's question as well," answered God, "we are all One and we think as one eternal entity. But you can understand that it is the Mind that links us all. If the Mind cannot think as united, then ascension is simply stopped temporarily. In your case, the next heartbeat will not occur in the human and you can all be One with Me. Then you can go Home, one step up into Universal Consciousness with Me. Remember, there are no conditions, punishments or judgments to be placed upon any of you. You are all eternal segments of the whole, learning your way to who you are. You are Me and I will not, and cannot, punish myself. You will all simply come Home with what you have learned and experienced, and decide whether you wish to remain Home or come back again to play out a new drama."

"And we will not forget what we know now?" asked Mind.

"My beautiful Mind," replied God, "you cannot unlearn what you have learned. What you know now will remain in your Consciousness, and hopefully you will draw out much, much more."

"And we can go back into the body and continue our lives?" asked Brain.

"Simply by Mind willing it to be so," replied God, "it has never been more difficult than that."

And so it came to be that the body awoke from its deathly state. The next heartbeat resounded through the surrounding equipment like a trumpet in the dead of night. And Ego, Brain, Soul, Mind, Heart, and the dear Chakra Children lived a long, happy, prosperous and fruitful life together in peace, harmony and without fear.

And so it was.

And so it is.

And so it will always be.

BOOK ABSTRACTS BY Ed Rychkun

The Secret Little Book: A New Age Prescription for a Great Life In this short little book, Ed Rychkun reveals what it has taken him "many lifetimes" to learn. He lays out a simple "down to earth" bottom line summary of the New Age. He then reveals his powerful secrets to a complete Body, Mind and Spirit Prescription for health and prosperity. In a simple, easy to read format, he summarizes his 8 Secret Truths of the Universe that have a direct affect on how you manifest a joyful life of abundance, harmony and love. Ed unfolds a simple Life Plan for everyone, then takes you on a quick journey of ascension and the New Age Great Awakening of 2012. This stunning Book will prepare you for a dynamic new future unfolding on this planet. *Take the New Age Prescription for a great life.*

The Book of Secrets: Breaking the Chains of your Spiritual and Commercial Bondage. In this book, Ed Rychkun tells a story about two happy Light Beings who volunteered for a special mission to planet Earth. Having been incarnated as Tom and Pam Doubtfull, they have been captured in a commercial and spiritual illusion that has consumed their existence. Live with them as they meet two Mentors and uncover the Secrets about the Cloak of the Matrix and how the truth has been hidden from them by the Global Elite. See how they cast away the old belief system to unplug from this Matrix. Learn the secrets of how they break their chains of Spiritual and Commercial bondage to walk through a new door into a new reality, and their New Age birthright. Learn how they **Wake up and unplug from the Spiritual and Commercial Illusion**.

Subtle Secrets: Talking Heart to Heart If you have ever had moments where you pondered why your life has unfolded the way it has and whether you had any control over making it better, you need to read this profound summary that combines ancient wisdom with recent scientific discoveries. In this book, Ed Rychkun gets to the "Heart" of how to manifest a life of quality time providing concise riveting information about why you need to start paying attention to the Subtle Laws of the Universe. These Subtle Laws reveal the common purpose of life transcending the boundaries of race and religious and spiritual differences so common on our conflictive planet. From the ancient wisdom of the ages, to the miracle healings of the religions, through New Age beliefs and from the most recent scientific discoveries, Ed extracts the essence of a common purpose and process with a resounding message: *"If you want to heal the planet, and generate love and peace, start with yourself and your own back yard. Then direct your mind to change your code of behavior to create coherence between the two main subtle energy centers - the heart and brain"*. **Take the action to manifest a quality life and activate your role to a peaceful planet.**

The Book of Secrets: Taking Back Your Financial and Spiritual Powers In this revealing book, Ed Rychkun continues the journey out of the Commercial and Spiritual Matrix imposed by the Global Elite. Learn astonishing secrets as Tom and Pam Doubtfull, two descended Light Beings who have now awakened from the deception of the Cloak of the Matrix, continue to dig deeper and deeper into the truth behind the Commercial and Spiritual Illusion. Learn how they create a Commercial Duality and recover the powers they have lost. In a compelling dialogue, Tom is subjected to the Commercial Martial Arts to earn his belts, each time opening a new door towards financial freedom. Here he uncovers new tactical secrets in the hidden private world of commerce to develop an arsenal of secret unpublished financial offensive and defensive weapons. See also how they transmute themselves spiritually by rejecting their Religious Duality to ultimately develop their new life plan leading them on their new journey towards ascension. ***Learn to take back your own financial and spiritual powers.***

Shift Happened: The Ubiquitology Handbook to the Peak Living Zone Take an exciting new journey into the new shift revolutionizing health care in this provocative handbook on Ubiquitology – healing by connecting mind and body with Spirit. Ronald Conn, a popular radio personality, and Founder of Ubiquity Wellness Centre, North America's foremost private preventative, natural wellness clinic, reveals how after his Near Death Experience he gave birth to his vision and has used revolutionary Ubiquitous healing methods to help thousands achieve their health and wellness goals. Learn how to stay in the Peak Living Zone as Ed Rychkun, former business executive, Reiki Master and Spiritual Writer takes you to the bottom line of how the Subtle Laws of the Universe work. He tells you why your life is the way it is, and how, by paying attention to the laws of subtle energies, manifesting a better quality life can become a reality. Together, Ronald and Ed provide a mind blowing handbook taking you onto the fast-track to optimum health and quality life through their simple Mind, Body and Spirit Code. ***Take the action to get into the Peak Living Zone.***

Commercial Martial Arts I: Taking off the Cloak of the Illuminati Matrix. In this work of fiction, Ed Rychkun explains how the Illuminati have captured Tom, a typical businessman, into their herd of Sheeple. He, like Nations, have unknowingly accepted the invisible Cloak of the Matrix that makes them and him a human capital machine working for a Strawman. Being siphoned by the commercial deception and fed the illusion of freedom, it is time for Tom to wake up. Understanding how bankrupt Nations have bonded him into paying for their folly, he wakes up to how this global deception has been implemented by the Global Elite. Watch as he takes off the Cloak and prepares himself for the Commercial Martial Arts. Learn the obscured, hidden secrets as Tom's Mentor leads him into the power of the Private World of Commerce, and how the Commercial and Spiritual Illusion can work for him. **Understand the Deception and take back your Private Freedoms.**

Commercial Martial Arts II: Taking Back Your Financial Powers In this work of fiction, Ed Rychkun takes you on a profound new journey through the commercial illusion. With the Cloak of the Matrix taken off, Tom is now able to learn his offensive and defensive weapons to take back his financial powers. As Tom's Mentor takes him through his Martial Arts lessons, he learns how to make the Strawman work for him and how to structure his financial affairs in the Private world of commerce. Through Tom's lessons, he learns how he can unplug from the legal, tax and banking siphons to take back his financial powers. Tom's tactical, unpublished secrets of deploying his new path towards Preparing, Privatizing and Protecting his financial world, changes his life forever. ***Bring the power of the private world of Commerce into your reality***.

The Book of Secrets: Preparing For Ascension In this book, Ed Rychkun continues the journey of ascension with Tom and Pam Doubtfull, two descended Light Beings who have awoken to who they really are. Having discovered how they have been captured into the commercial and spiritual illusions, they now know exactly how to unplug from the Cloak of the Matrix and take back their spiritual and financial powers. Now Tom and Pam must set a practical new course that takes them through a Life Plan and back to their lineage of Spirit – their birthright. Follow Pam and Tom as they now lay out their steps of ascending from their 3D material conundrum into 4D and 5D light beings, crossing over the 2012 zero point predicted by the Mayans. Learn how they rationalize the conflicting prophesies, galactic cataclysms, Earth upheaval, and economic collapse using New Age, scientific, biblical and esoteric evidence to determine their ultimate plan. Follow them in their struggle to go back to Nature, leave the material world behind and prepare for their final homecoming. ***Prepare yourself for Ascension and the Great Awakening.***

Xolani and the Magic Shanty In this Adult/Children's book, Ed Rychkun tells the story of Xolani, an angry 12 year old Zulu boy living in Shanty Town in South Africa. Life is not good here and he has taken up with a band of ruffians to get back at the wealthy and the Whites whom they have learned to hate. One day Xolani finds a Magic Shanty and meets and unusual Nharo Medicine Man. Xolani finds he is not as bad as he thought and some of his Crystal Child characteristics are making life a conflict.

Suddenly life begins to change for him and the people around him as he begins to blossom, and he learns how he can make his own Magic Shanty. Follow his life changing experience in the poverty stricken Shanty Town as he changes his and everyone else's life. Shanty Town will never be the same. **Live with Xolani as he unfolds his new destiny**

Jack and the Great Oak Tree In this enlightening and fascinating Adult/Children's book, Ed Rychkun weaves a story of a boy and girl that on the surface appears as a fairy tale, yet has a profound message about the relationship of Crystal Children, their environment, and their parents. Jack is an eight year old Crystal boy who does not seem to fit in with much of anything "normal". He has no friends, hates school and seems to be dysfunctional to his parents. But Jack loves to be One with Nature and has some secret skills. He sees people's auras and he smells things differently. He can read other's thoughts. He talks to animals and trees, and he hates fake things like the Zombie Box his parents watch. He dislikes conflict and dishonesty, and can read the energy of it. He rejects plastic junk toys other kids love. What must the parents do to him to make him normal becomes Jack's and their dilemma. But one day Jack finds a giant magic Oak Tree in the deep forest. It changes his life, and the others around him forever. Follow Jack as his adventures lead him to knowing who he really is and what he, and his parents must do in their lives. **Join Jack and Suzie in the most life changing adventure of their lives**.

Rychkun's Laws of AQ'ISM Want a fresh, new humorous look at the business world we all live in? Take a tour of corporate life through Ed Rychkun's view of his lifetime of climbing corporate ladders. This provocative and hilarious expose' shows what really goes on behind those boardroom walls. It reveals the flip side of a company's naked underbelly by showing how people universally conform to laws on how they feel about each other called AQ'ISM – a classification of "Asshole". Ed examines the social behavior of corporate citizens and develops his universal laws about how this feeling is quantified as an AQ, and how it can have a direct impact on how fast you can climb or fall from the corporate ladder. Ed tells it like it is, revealing how the "real" professionals - the Executives, use a set of secret AQ Arsenals to hide their incompetence - and maintain their positions of power in the corporate hierarchy. You will immediately recognize a similarity with your own situation and derive humor from it. But beware… as one critic points out, *"Never was the raw naked truth so aptly expressed as in this earthy examination of the blatantly exposed underbelly of the modern corporation".* **Learn how to avoid being a Corporate Asshole!**

Fast-Track Self Publishing: Manifesting Your Passions Here is a provocative new twist on publishing your own book. Ed Rychkun, Author, and Self-Publisher of over 20 books, takes you onto the fast-track highway of low cost, demand publishing world of the Internet. Completely bypassing publishers, printers, and traditional manuscript methods, Ed shows you how to get your passion in professional, printed book form for less than a few hundred dollars - and get that and more back from tax savings. Then in a most revealing twist on marketing, Ed takes you on an enlightening journey of how to take your favourite passions and use these to build your book publishing into a private enterprise at virtually no cost. Follow Ed as he explains how to create marketing energy behind your success of self publishing. No, you do not need to print and pay for an inventory of books. No, you do not need to hire expensive design artists. No you do not need to pay for editing and expensive publicists. Yes, you can write off against income your costs of following your passions. **See if you can manifest your own passion.**

Who Said Fishing Was Serious? Here is the best fishing and fireside companion you could ask for. This book is full of short fishing stories that started out serious but turned into funny, gut-wrenching calamities. You will be amazed at the crazy situations that Ed has selected. Focusing on stories that pit the large brained angler against that small pea-brained fish, Ed will have you in stitches as he and his brother take to the challenge. See if you can contain yourself when you read the events that unfold in his short stories. How many times has your own technical assault on those little fish turned into a side-splitting laughing frenzy? Checkout Ed's special selection of not so serious fishing mis-adventures taken from his many years of fishing for that BIG ONE. **Who Said Fishing Was Serious?** is a refreshing experience into laughter. See if you can contain yours. **See how serious you take fishing after indulging in these stories.**

A Private Limited Liability

www.edrychkun.com

www.ingramcontent.com/pod-product-compliance
Lightning Source LLC
Chambersburg PA
CBHW051700090426
42736CB00013B/2467